Shattered Reflections

A Dark and Melancholic Poetic Anthology

Ananditha Sreejit Warrier

BookLeaf Publishing

India | USA | UK

The Publisher and Editor shall not be liable whatsoever...

Made with ❤ on the BookLeaf Publishing Platform
www.bookleafpub.in
www.bookleafpub.com

*To all those enduring difficult times, this book is a
beacon for you.*

*May you find solace in knowing you are never
truly alone in this world.*

Acknowledgement

Profound gratitude for the experiences that have inspired me in ways I never imagined. Thank you to all who were there for me, offering understanding and support during my journey.

A special thanks to my dear readers and to all who have guided me through my poetic journey.

Your support and appreciation have never gone unnoticed and will forever hold a special place in my heart.

Preface

"Shattered Reflections: A Dark and Melancholic Poetic Anthology" is a short collection of poems inspired by the struggles we all face in our lives. This book aims to portray the complexities of human life—those moments we tend to hide, the feelings we keep inside, the thoughts we do not let out. As you venture through these poems, you might find instances that resonate with you, feelings you relate to. At the end of the day, everyone in this universe is bound together. All those around the world share your griefs and your joys in some way or another. It is what makes humans human.

Silent Heartbreak

She penned her soul in ink,
He devoured each word,
Her sorrows and her joys,
In his heart, they stirred.

She wrote late at night,
He would read them at dawn,
She sprawled by the fire,
He studied by the lawn.

She wondered who could like,
Her simple pieces of fiction,
He pondered on who could write,
Such classics with perfection.

Little did they know,
The other was always there,
One's source of inspiration,
The other's motivation.

The wordsmith wrote,
From her heart, he had broke,
The latter read,
To escape his feelings, she awoke.

The Grave

At the brink of the end of time,
Before their eyes flashes more than a day,
they sit yet at the gateways of their grave,
As though it is a breath they gave away.

They sit whining in their blood,
tears stream as death awaits,
yet what would they know,
Gone away are the dates.

They ponder on where they are,
the place they set from gone from sight,
A streak of light sails to their side,
Horrors they think but truly not quite.

They find the light bless their soul,
heartache a second gave,
now it is done, gone away,
for now they have left their grave.

Lost in Shadows of Memory

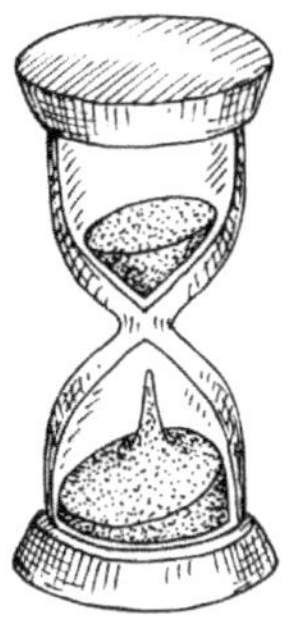

She keeps on thinking,
Of the days long gone,
Those moments, now memories,
Calling time a con.

She was always afraid,
Of losing the past,
That it was never on her mind,
To not leave today behind.

She would forever reflect,
On all that was over,
She never gave time,
To enjoy her prime.

Crosses on her calendar,
Until one brand new,
When each emotion passed,
Nostalgia settled anew.

She mourned her losses,
And never acknowledged her gain,
Her life never felt fulfilled,
With simply void and pain.

Then came that day,
She cried of agony,
Not because the day was over,
But since it brought tragedy.

When remorse ran through,
And she finally could see,
How blind she had been,
To each day's gentle plea.

She no longer would reflect,
On all the time prior,
And she no longer could fret,
For she learned from her regret.

Desolation

Oh, where am I,
Where is this place I reside,
So deserted, so empty,
With nowhere to hide.

In this loud, noisy world,
It is just another day,
Where somewhere deep down,
I am floating away.

I know not what I say,
I know not what I feel,
Is this all even true,
Are my thoughts even real?

I look around just to find,
Faces smiling with glee,
The sad with a shoulder to rest on,
And then there's lonely little me.

I often stop to think,
Is there a point to my existence,
Anything I am meant to do,
Perhaps I could be of assistance.

When everyone seems content,
And with my life I try to cope,
Each time I see someone's joy,
I simply rid myself of all hope.

Things that once made me beam,
Could no longer matter,
Those who I once held at heart,
Far off, I hear them chatter.

Some people often ask,
"Why do you find comfort in isolation?"
Truth is, there's nothing comforting,
For this is mere desolation.

Veil of Suffering

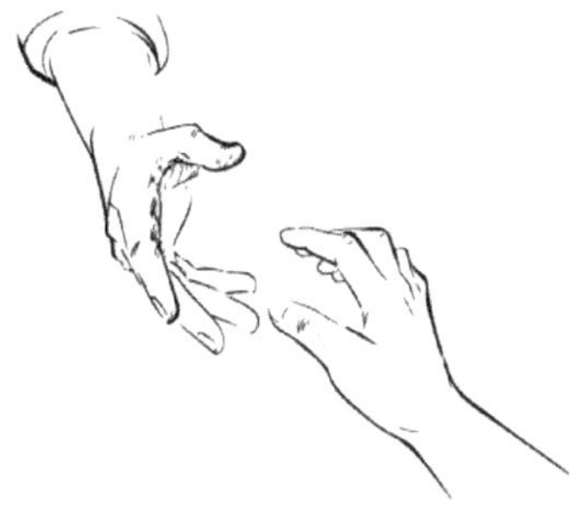

Young by both soul and time,
They were of hearts so pure,
Punished by this cruel world,
Had too much left to endure.

Sewed by the Moirai,
Is a life they would hate,
Of none but rejection,
Lost spirits; their fate.

Starts at their home,
Then sneers from a friend,
Colleagues, and neighbors,
The list has no end.

They feel all alone,
As though no one is there,
To lend them a hand,
And show that they care.

They are not in the wrong,
For it is time that we spread,
A little bit kindness before,
They break and see red.

You just might say,
That no one is around,
So lonely, so deserted,
Forgotten year round.

But have you ever,
Paused to reflect,
That some souls you see,
Hang on by a thread?

Perhaps that salesmen,
Or a friend you had snapped at,
Maybe even a coworker,
Or even a dog or a cat.

Whoever it is,
A bit of benevolence,
Will always bring a smile,
For those used to malevolence.

The Weight of Words

You might just think,
That a harmless joke,
Or a tiny comment,
Couldn't ever poke.

But when it comes to you,
What is it you say ?
Oh that it isn't funny,
There is a price you should pay?

Do you even understand,
That what may seem silly,
Creates scars that last,
For all of eternity?

You'll probably say,
It is not even that deep,
But every single word,
In the heart it shall seep.

They could take it,
Far from what you mean,
To them what happened,
A completely different scene.

So next time you'll say,
A thing or two to them,
Perhaps think it twice,
And let 'em sparkle, a gem

A single compliment,
Before it is too late,
Can fix what was broken,
To respect, from hate.

Behind those Cheerful Eyes

Full of cheer,
Happiest of all,
She smiled at rainbows,
Winter and fall.

She was there for those disheartened,
To pick up those who fell down,
She always knew what to do,
To bring a grin from a frown.

If anyone was ever alone,
She'd drag them by her side,
Make sure they were alright,
Oh what a lovely sight.

Surely she is this way,
Because her life is perfect,
Or is it a misconception,
A terrible misinterpretation?

If you look closely,
You would perhaps fathom,
Those passionate eyes,
Hide the false phantasm.

It is correct, she never told,
Her pain she hid deep down,
But every time she made you smile,
Did you notice her frown?

Whenever she ensured you're fine,
Did you ever treat her that way?
Check up on how she was feeling,
Ask, how was her day?

If you haven't yet,
Well now is the time to start,
She deserves it too,
It is time you play your part.

For behind those cheerful eyes,
Lies a story deep and vast,
Let's honor her silent battles,
And make her joy last.

The Sun's Dark Side

People tend to think,
That I am a happy soul,
For I am seen by all,
With a very important role.

I give light in the day,
Get to rest at night,
When I am there,
No one shall fright.

They do not see,
That there is a dark side to me,
One that you can't imagine,
And it pokes me, like a pin.

Though I eliminate darkness,
You praise my twin's perfection,
And don't acknowledge my beauty,
Even though she is my reflection.

Then when I provide,
A way to see,
You hide in shelter,
And complain about me.

When I give a rainbow,
You say it's thanks to the rain,
But do you not notice,
My sufferings, my pain?

Alas I must be,
The cheery celestial object,
A master of positivity,
Joy I must project.

The Art of Being You

Not all of us are flawless,
We all aren't pretty,
Some of us fail to impress,
Other's standards, so petty.

Those who are blessed,
With such perfection,
May never know the grace,
Of true affection.

It's funny don't you think,
How life is the same?
Regardless of one's opinion,
Whatever is their claim.

If you fit in the box,
That is all that shall be seen,
As for those who don't,
Their presence goes unseen.

So what is the point in trying,
To be the perfect picture,
When no matter the portrait,
You shan't ever be the main feature.

Because of his own paintings,
We know of Van Gough,
Because of his sculptures,
We speak of Picasso.

We do not hear of the others,
Those who forged what they see,
Nothing of their own,
No originality.

Soon we shall get weary,
If we see the same old paintings,
The same pieces every day,
Nothing new to say.

All there is to tell,
Is to be you while you can,
For duplicates and copies,
Don't have a loyal fan.

An Inevitable Choice

I never really wanted,
To be put in such a state,
Where I had to say those words,
But impending was my fate.

It is not my fault,
That the time had come,
But I feel so guilty,
My senses, so numb.

They all told me,
To make the right decision,
And I knew what I did,
Had the utmost precision.

Yet there is this pin,
That pokes my head,
Not giving reassurance,
But regret instead.

I am well aware,
My intentions were good,
My actions justified,
To most understood.

It is only to myself,
That I must convince,
To not dwell too much,
My judgment, my province.

As I say these words,
I prove I am conscious,
That my deeds are proper,
That I need not be anxious.

Oh, what a tale of mine,
I say with such sentiments,
The kind hard to comprehend,
Like a cacophony of instruments.

Despite my anguish,
I must laugh at my own story,
An inevitable choice,
Oh what an irony.

Fabrications of Failure

"Failure teaches success",
"Learn from your mistakes",
But how many should I make,
For none more can I take.

They say good things take time,
But how long should I wait?
I've been patient long enough,
I won't fall for the bluff.

"Fall seven times, stand up eight."
I fell down seven, then fell back eight,
Falling this much, soon I shall collapse,
I'd say this is all a lie, perhaps.

He who makes no mistakes,
Is said to make nothing,
Well that is all I've ever made,
Yet why am I not left with something?

What do you mean,
"Failure is a stepping stone to success"?
It is just a boulder crashing down,
Leaving me in utter distress.

"Every failure is a lesson.",
That cannot be true,
If it was then it would mean,
I am the smartest person ever seen.

"Slow and steady wins the race,"
Yet haste is often praised as grace.
"Good things come to those who wait,"
But the impatient dominate our fate.

Our hearts yearn for the truth,
Amidst the trials of our youth,
Proverbs spoken far and wide,
Often leaves us mystified.

Could someone please let me know,
How much further they shall grow,
These falsehoods you teach us,
Planting seeds of mistrust.

"Failure is the path to success,"
Sounds more like a cruel jest.
Why must we bear these riddles and rhymes,
When life's struggles, don't fit the times?

Genders Justified

You say "She's a sweetheart",
And that "He's a tough guy",
It does not seem wrong,
Yet it's time to question why.

Can only the gentle be kind,
And the strong be brave?
Men must fight,
While women behave?

Everything is deadly,
Everything is precious,
How you perceive it,
One must be cautious.

For sparks can burn,
The ocean can drown,
Grounds can crumble,
Winds can tear one down.

Yet even flames can warm,
Rain can help grow,
The trees protect,
As air lets life flow.

Boys can cry,
Girls can be bold,
It is time to open our eyes,
And break the mold.

Strength knows no gender,
Kindness knows no face,
In every heart, there's a blend,
Of power and grace.

Times of Yore

I wonder if you recall those times,
Moments of joy, filled with glee,
Those cherished memories,
Of both you and me.

Oh how I yearn for the times of yore,
Our exchange of whispers, I long for more.

I remember the jokes we cracked,
The way we teased each other,
But those teases are now sneers,
The kind from which it's hard to recover.

Oh how I yearn for the times of yore,
The pranks we pulled, I long for more.

As I see you every day,
With your friends along the way,
I recall our bond so tight,
Wishing our camaraderie stayed bright.

Oh how I yearn for the times of yore,
The thoughts we'd share, I long for more.

I am not aware of what happened,
Did we drift, or did we rift,
But one thing I know for sure,
Is I miss your company, a gift.

Oh how I yearn for the times of yore,
Though I know there shan't be any more.

Fractured Faith

I put all my faith in you,
I spent every dime on you,
But is there any point in what I did,
When you proceed to act like a kid?

I gave you all that I could,
I helped you feel understood,
I helped you become who you are,
Made you a shining star.

All my struggles I did not show,
All my pain, you did not know,
I hid it all to let you free,
And this is how you repay me.

Your best interests lay in my heart,
As you tear my life apart,
Just as I let you shimmer bright,
You left me on the coldest night.

I did everything in my power,
For you to bloom into a flower,
But little did I know this seed,
Would soon grow into a weed.

That is it, I've had enough,
For fake vows, I am no buff,
No more patience for empty words,
Unheard cries, like distant birds.

Brightest Dreams

We looked outside windows,
Pointed at the stars,
Said we'd be astronauts,
On our way to mars.

Do you recall those times we let out joyful
screams?
Voices echoing as we praised our brightest
dreams.

Once we made a painting,
Colors we cleverly mixed,
Dreaming to be artists,
Our visions were fixed.

Do you recall those times we let out joyful
screams?
Voices echoing as we praised our brightest
dreams.

Shortly after we announced,
Our big plans for the future,
From an author it would change,
To pursuing architecture.

Do you recall those times we let out joyful
screams?
Voices echoing as we praised our brightest
dreams.

Nonetheless, we were carefree,
Changes of all kinds to bring,
From heroes to emperors,
We could be anything.

Do you recall those times we let out joyful
screams?
Voices echoing as we praised our brightest
dreams.

But now it seems all gone,
Our spirit seems to be faded,
Why is it this way,
When we once felt elated?

Do you recall those times we let out joyful
screams?
Voices echoing as we praised our brightest
dreams.

Second Chances

They ask for another day,
In which the slack away,
And then they come back,
Empty promises they stack.

And yet why do you do this?
Thinking it's them you'll miss,
You try to bring peace,
And think this all shall cease.

It's a new story each week,
A flu, a test, till a mountain peak,
They say it is the last time,
But to them you don't mean a dime.

A second chance leads to a third,
Until they're gone away like a bird,
You waste your time forgiving,
When they do you not even some thinking.

Till when will it go on?
When shall you move on?
You'll keep on giving till you get none,
And they'll leave you when their job is done.

You musn't wait behind,
You have a future left to find,
Being the last one people see,
Shan't get you where you ought to be.

Repeating the same deeds tomorrow,
Shall only leave you with sorrow,
Keep flipping the same pages,
And to open a new book it'll take ages.

I Should've

I Should've done something I didn't.
I Should've said something I couldn't

I always think to fix what I broke,
To stop what I myself awoke,
I go back towards the past,
And mourn when I should have a blast.

I Should've done something I didn't.
I Should've said something I couldn't

I ponder endlessly,
About the things long gone,
I keep worrying,
From twilight to dawn.

I Should've done something I didn't.
I Should've said something I couldn't

I tell myself to look ahead,
Away from sunset, to sunrise instead,
But all I get myself to see,
Is the shadow lingering behind me.

I Should've done something I didn't.
I Should've said something I couldn't

I know how much it affects me,
I know I should just let things be,
But then again it's the same everyday,
The same old verse I proceed to say,

"I Should've done something I didn't.
I Should've said something I couldn't."

Their Broken Promise

She sees smug smiles,
Odd glances her way,
And many more things,
She'd rather not say.

He hear the things they say,
All behind his back,
Though he doesn't understand,
These rumors they stack.

They've done nothing to no one,
Kept quiet as always,
Never let a tear drop fall,
And didn't look up in the hallways.

She always kept their secrets,
Never spilled a bean,
And yet here she wonders,
Why is everyone so mean.

He acts like he doesn't know,
As clueless as can be,
He pretends he doesn't care,
Says, "Nothing can break me."

But you see, that isn't true,
Life paints a different view,
What they say, isn't their reality.
For everything affects them deeply,

She overthinks way too much,
Because she's afraid of being judged,
Scared of what you think,
Her thoughts hence being nudged.

He tells himself every day,
To let it all slide,
To just be himself,
And have nothing to hide.

As much as they hate to admit,
It is just the sad honest fact,
They break it everyday,
Their daily depressing pact.

The pact that she'll be honest,
The vow that he won't hide anything,
The oath they made to themselves,
The promise that they've been breaking.

They hope they'll be able to say,
That they've finally kept what they'd sworn,
That they've finally spent a day,
Without being mentally worn.

Lost and Found

When there's nothing left to say,
No more to be done,
A heart poured out,
It is empty; none to shout.

No cries to write,
No laughs to draw,
Just an empty mind,
No good, no flaw.

An artist without paper,
A musician without music,
A dancer without beats that sink,
A poet without any ink.

What more could one do,
When one has not a clue,
Things that came so quickly,
Now lost for eternity.

Yet they have what it takes,
Each gifted soul,
To go back once more,
And reach their goal.

The artist knows their paint,
The musician knows their notes,
The dancer knows their rhythm,
And the poet knows their quotes.

And so, they find their way back,
To the place they hold dear,
Starting their renewed journey,
Like a sailor, to shores so near.

Narratives of Nighttime

As the day begins to retire,
And the night has begun,
As we are tucked into bed,
Dreams start to run.

In that fleeting moment,
What do you suppose takes place,
In the house down the lane,
Is it trouble, or solace?

The one so cheery at dawn,
Need not be so at dusk,
The other who seemed so weary,
Could now be ready to busk.

What about those asleep,
The ones deep in their slumbers,
What do you think goes in their head,
As the night slowly lumbers.

Do they dream of places,
They wish to explore,
Or of the people,
They most adore?

All said, it is the same,
Eyes be covered or eyes be not,
Each have their own stories,
All have their own plot.

In the quiet of the night,
When the world is at rest,
Our thoughts take flight,
And journeys manifest.

So let the night embrace us,
With its gentle, soothing touch,
For in the quiet moments,
We find so very much.

Sorrow Strengthens

Far from what eyes can see,
Locked away, without a key,
Were emotions we tucked inside,
Thoughts to none we'd confide.

So used to those endless nights,
Triggered by daytime's plights,
We cried ourselves to sleep,
Until no longer, could we weep.

Those busy days we'd stress over,
Wishing we had a four leaved clover,
No time to take a simple break,
For we knew there was lots at stake.

In this moment however,
There is this feeling not felt, ever.
Like something has changed,
Feel as though we've become deranged.

No longer do we think of things prior,
Now we think of ourselves higher,
With dreams that set our souls on fire,
A newfound strength that can not tire.

It is a lie to say we now miss,
Those old sorrows, replaced by bliss,
Yet part of ourselves feels missing,
In this new dawn, we're reminiscing.

Though we feel more content,
When our grief began to descent,
It shall forever play its part,
Etched deeply within our heart.

For it's in our scars that strength is found,
And in our trials, resilience crowned,
We move forward, with courage anew,
Knowing our past has shaped our view.